9 SOURCES OF NATURAL OILS AND THEIR BENEFITS.

Utilizing the beauty of natural oil

By

Dr DOUGLAS JASON

TABLE OF CONTENTS

TABLE OF CONTENTS

CHAPTER 9
Sesame

CONCLUSION

ABOUT THE AUTHOR

Dr DOUGLAS JASON is a certified dietician who has a strong passion for wellness and a big eagerness to help people all over the world. He uses healthy food, herbs, sauce and other useful tools to help mankind realize its overall goal of optimum health.

INTRODUCTION

Natural oil are promoted as substitutes for products that strengthen nails, hydrate skin, condition hair, and treat acne. You can discover them in a variety of items if you take a stroll down the beauty aisle of your local drugstore. Do they operate? You may need to conduct certain tests. Because every person's skin is unique, it boils down to trial and error.

Natural oils have been utilized for millennia for a variety of uses, including cooking, aromatherapy, and skincare and haircare. These oils, which come from plants and other organic sources, are full of advantageous substances that have many benefits for our health. In this post, we'll examine some popular natural oil sources and delve into the amazing advantages they offer. These oils are now a crucial part of our daily routines because of their numerous health and wellness benefits, including hydrating and nourishing the skin.

CHAPTER 1

MARULA

This oil is moisturizing and made from the fruit of the marula tree, which is indigenous to South Africa. Fatty acids, which are abundant in it, physicians claim alleviate dry skin. It immediately absorbs and leaves you feeling matted and ungreasy.

CHAPTER 2

TEA TREE

When germs become caught in your pores, it causes red, inflammatory breakouts. According to research, tea tree oil helps kill bacteria. It outperformed a placebo gel (which contains no active ingredients) in a study on the treatment of acne and inflammation. According to a different study, it is equally as effective as benzoyl peroxide, a frequent component in over-the-counter acne treatments.

CHAPTER 3

ARGAN.

The antioxidants known as polyphenols, which are abundant in argan oil and are sometimes referred to as "liquid gold," can help combat the signs of aging. Additionally, omega-3 fatty acids are said by dermatologists to promote collagen formation and fill up your skin. Whether you have dry, oily, or normal skin doesn't matter.

Additionally, it conditions hair without making it feel greasy or weighing it down. You can still utilize the rest of your hair care supplies.

Chapter 4

Peppermint and Chamomile

Although you generally associate chamomile with calming tea, the oil from this plant that resembles a daisy can also soothe your skin. It reduces inflammation, irritation, and the risk of infection, which is why dermatologists refer to it as both an anti-inflammatory and an antiseptic. The same calming effects can be found in peppermint oil.

CHAPTER 5

COCONUT

Skin that is dry and cracked is more prone to infection, irritation, and allergic responses. The scaly, rough patches that are associated with common illnesses like eczema are also soothed by coconut oil, which also hydrates and protects the skin.

CHAPTER 6

ROSEHIP AND CARROT

Vitamin A is present in numerous skin care products. It is a "retinoid," a substance that produces collagen and aids in the production of new skin cells, which can lessen color changes brought on by scarring and stretch marks. Rosehip seed and carrot oils are particularly high in vitamin A. They are also effective as anti-aging and acne treatments, according to

certain specialists. At night,
you would simply use a tiny
dab.

CHAPTER 7

ROSEMARY AND CASTOR

Want to make your ponytail fuller? Does your scalp protrude more than usual? You could get a thicker, glossier mane with rosemary oil. In one trial, 2% minoxidil and six months of therapy were equally effective in treating androgenetic alopecia, a frequent cause of hair loss in both men and women. It was also less likely to result in a scratchy scalp.

Another natural treatment for thickening brows and lashes is castor oil. Since it would be close to your eyes, ask your doctor if it is safe before using it. Whether it works is still up for debate.

CHAPTER 8

AVOCADO AND OLIVE

Have you got brittle or thin nails? Apply some olive or avocado oil to them before bed for an easy, natural fix. Overnight, the oils will absorb and provide nourishing fatty acids. For this, you can also use various kinds of oil.

CHAPTER 9

Sesame

Could you use oil instead of mouthwash? Oil pulling, or washing your mouth with oil, is a time-honored method for maintaining healthy teeth and gums. It might help, according to research. Sesame oil (coconut and sunflower oil also work) mouthwash has been shown in recent international research to reduce plaque and gingivitis. The bacteria that cause bad breath could also be washed away by it.

CONCLUSION

Natural oils come from a wide range of sources and have numerous advantages for our general health. These oils, which can be made from seeds, nuts, fruits, or flowers, have demonstrated their effectiveness in several industries, including skincare, haircare, and even culinary uses. Since ancient times, societies all around the world have valued the moisturizing, nourishing, and healing qualities that the natural molecules in these oils offer. Natural oils' appeal in aromatherapy practices is also a result of their therapeutic properties, which improve relaxation and foster emotional well-being. Understanding each oil's unique properties will help us choose the right ones to meet our unique needs as we continue to explore the potential of natural oils. We can uncover natural oils' incredible benefits and provide our bodies and minds with natural nourishment by

incorporating them into our
regular routines.